How to Spray Paint Furniture
-A guide for beginners-

Nick van der Walt

Copyright © 2016 Nick van der Walt

All rights reserved.

ISBN:1537349732
ISBN-13:9781537349732

CONTENTS

Introduction

1. Tools and equipment

2. Types of paints, primers and sealers

3. How to prepare the wood for painting

4. Spray painting basics

5. How to spray paint different wood surfaces

6. Resources

Conclusion

INTRODUCTION

Painted furniture has become a popular trend and by using the right tools, paints and other materials and paint techniques, you can give new life to a piece of furniture. Spray painting furniture is by far the best way to go about it because it is much quicker than painting with a brush or a roller and the end result so much more rewarding. Whether a beginner or a more experienced furniture painter, in this book you will find a detailed guide on aspects such as the best tools and equipment for spray painting, what types of paint to use, how to prepare wood for painting, the basics of the technique of spray painting etc. There is also a section dealing with the best approach to paint different types of wood surfaces such as hardwood, laminated wood and MDF (medium density fiber) and how to spray chalk paint and milk paint. You will find many useful practical tips and suggestions to get you started to become a master spray painter. Whether you are just starting out by using an ordinary spray can or using a handheld sprayer or want to progress to a more professional level of using a spray gun with a compressor – this book covers all the necessary aspects to get you there. Spray painting can be mastered with relative ease and your projects can achieve a new level of sophistication in no time. I hope you will enjoy this book and that you will find it informative and useful.

1. TOOLS AND EQUIPMENT

Painting furniture, like any other trade, can only be done properly with the right tools and equipment. Although tools such as brushes and rollers are used most frequently for painting furniture, the technological advancement of paint sprayers has made it relatively easy and cheap to achieve a professional end result. Sprayers have so many advantages over brushes and rollers that more people are using some type of spray equipment for DIY purposes. That said there still is a place for old fashioned brushes and rollers for painting and decorating furniture and other objects. My own preference is to use a compressed air spray system because it is relatively easy to master the technique of spraying and it gives you a truly professional finish. However, other options will also be discussed.

1.1 Equipment for spray painting

To get started with paint spraying the following tools and equipment can get you started:

- Air compressor
- Spray gun(s)
- Safety gear
- Mixing tools

Other tools and equipment include:

- Sanding equipment such as a hand orbital sander and belt sander
- Paint brushes, rollers and paint scrapers
- Hand tools such as a screw driver, hammer, pliers etc
- Power tools such as a drill, planer, power saw etc.

1.1.1 Compressors

To start off with I would suggest that a small compressor be acquired. A minimum tank capacity of 50 L is required. It should be driven by a motor of at least 2 hp or 1.5 kW. An air delivery rate of minimum 6 cfm (cubic feet per minute) and maximum pressure of 8 bars or 116 psi (pounds per square inch) is needed. This size compressor will easily handle most HVLP guns but because of the small tank capacity and high air consumption rate of the HVLP gun, will run out of air when spraying bigger surfaces. This means that you will have to interrupt spraying for a few minutes in order for the compressor to get the pressure up again. With a small compressor you are limited to smaller jobs. As an alternative you could consider an electric turbine driven sprayer for smaller jobs.

Should the volume of work increase, a bigger and more expensive compressor is essential and the smaller compressor can then be used as stand-by or used for on-site jobs. A tank capacity of 100 liter and 7 to 8 cfm clean air delivery rate will be adequate.

There are two advantages to using a compressor driven spray gun over an airless turbine spray gun:

> A compressor that is large enough (2-5 horsepower) can generate more pressure at the gun than do commonly available turbines-up to 10 psi. This results into more finish material being deposited onto the wood surface at a faster rate. The increase allows you to coat an object in less time. Turbine supplied HVLP spray guns don't put out as much material as compressor-supplied HVLP guns or, for that matter, compressor supplied conventional guns.

> A compressor can be used for other shop tasks, such as powering compressed-air woodworking tools and blowing dust off your work. Turbines are ineffective at these tasks.

1.1.2 Spray guns

> A spray gun is the only tool that will give you a professional finish. It will give a really smooth finish whereas brushes and rollers always leave marks. It's estimated that a paint sprayer can apply a coating ten times faster than brushing and four times faster than rolling. Paint sprayers give a uniform finish and are easy use in tight areas.

There are three common types of DIY spray guns used in finishing:

> Conventional **air spray guns** come in versions of Low Volume High Pressure (LVHP) operated with compressed air that blasts the finish

onto the wood at 3.5 – 5.0 bars and the High Volume Low Pressure (HVLP) operating at 1.5 to 3 Bar at an air delivery rate of 7 to 12 cfm.

The second category refers to **airless spray guns**. These guns do not require compressed air since the paint is delivered via an electric motor powered by a turbine(s) or by building up high pressure in the apparatus and the air supply hose. They will spray latex or oil based paints as well as water based paints and primers, varnishes, stains etc. The pressurized versions are designed to spray walls, floors and ceilings and are not very effective for smaller items such as furniture. They have been around for a long time and are very expensive.

A third category has appeared on the market in the recent past. These are airless guns but they do not operate under high pressure as the older type airless guns. These are the **electric driven turbine assisted airless spray guns.** They have been specifically designed for the DIY market and are easy to operate. The Wagner W550 and Graco hand held sprayers are good examples of good low pressure electric spray guns. They are also HVLP guns and can spray almost all types of paint and in most cases the paint need not be thinned. Although spray quality is not as good as compressed air sprayers, they are not too expensive and perfect for the beginner.

Low Volume High Pressure Spray Guns (LVHP)

Conventional high spray guns have been used for a long time. They provide excellent control of the liquid material that reaches the surface. But they have one serious drawback - they are only about 20 to 30 percent efficient. This means that well over half of the material you're spraying is wasted - it goes into the air.

These guns operate at high pressure of 5 to 7 bar and an air consumption rate of 12 cfm. They are manly used in the motor industry.

High Volume Low Pressure Spray Guns (HVLP)

HVLP spray guns were developed more than 30 years ago but only recently becoming popular. HVLP guns can work with either compressed air or continuous air supplied by a turbine. Either way, the result is a low pressure spray that creates very little overspray. HVLP guns are 65 to 90 percent efficient, which means that most of the material you're spraying ends up on the wood. These guns typically operate at 40 psi or 2.8 Bar with an air consumption rate of 8 to 12 cfm. HVLP can lay the finish onto the wood softly with minimum overspray.

There are **2 advantages** in using an **airless turbine assisted gun**:

> Turbines warm and dry the air, which speeds curing of the paint and helps reduce blushing (a moisture-related, off-white color that appears as some finishes cure).
>
> Turbines do not need a compressor and is much cheaper than a compressed air system

Compressed air HVLP guns have the following advantages:

> HVLP guns require low pressure and therefore have very little overspray. It delivers a much smoother layer of paint and a higher quality finish. They do however require a high air delivery rate and require a compressor that will deliver enough air.
>
> Modern HVLP guns can effectively spray a wide range of paints such as Acrylic and oil based paints.
>
> They deliver paint much faster and save time.

Recommendation:

If you are only starting out with spraying and will use a spray gun only occasionally, the DIY electric airless spray gun will meet most of your requirements. Should you want to get more serious it will pay you to get a small compressor and a HVLP gun with a 2.0 mm nozzle for general painting. My personal choice is to have a gravity feed rather than a suction feed gun.

With a HVLP gun you will need an air compressor with the following minimum specification:

>Tank size: 100 liter
>Motor size: 3 hp or 2.2 kW
>Clean air delivery rate: 7 to 8 cfm
>Maximum pressure: 116 psi or 8 bar.

1.1.3 Safety gear

Working with paint and solvents can be hazardous to your health. Spray painting produces toxic overspray and should be avoided as far as possible. Luckily there is wide variety safety equipment available and if you use it wisely, will ensure that you are adequately protected.

The following items are considered to be the minimum requirement:

>Respirator
>Safety glasses
>Protective clothing
>Ear protection
>Adequate ventilation

1.1.3.1 Respirators

There are many types of respirators available on the market but to my mind the 3M products are by far the best and although more expensive will provide maximum protection.

Respirators come in a wide range of types and sizes.

They range from cheaper disposable types to reusable types that make use of replaceable filtering cartridges.

The two main categories are:

>Air purifying respirator (APR)
>Air supplied respirator (SAR)

APR's forces contaminated air through a cartridge filter that contains an absorbing material such as carbon and the gases and fumes are absorbed. They are tight fitting and are available in different forms:

Quarter mask – covers nose and mouth

Half - face mask – covers face from the nose to below the chin

Full face mask – covers face from the eyes to below the chin. It protects the eyes from dust and fumes.

SAR's supply clean air from a compressed air tank. The air from a tank must comply with standards for purity and moisture. These systems are mostly used in industrial applications and are expensive. For a home business the half- or full-face mask APR systems are more than adequate.

The best filter to use is the type that combines the chemical filter with a particle filter.

3M Filter cartridges

3M Particulate filters protect against dust, mists, fumes, aerosols, smoke, mould, bacteria etc.

3M Gas- and vapor cartridge filters protects against different kinds of gasses and vapors. There are different types of filters for different kind of gasses.

3M Combination filters protect against particles and vapors.

Filters must be checked regularly to make sure it does not become clogged. Cartridges have a limited life span and must be replaced when they become saturated. It will stop working when the filters start to let contaminant through once their absorbents become saturated. When this happens you will start smelling and tasting the paint vapor. The best is to follow the manufacturer's recommendations. Cartridge filters must be replaced when:

    The paint vapor can be smelled or tasted

    The filters have been used for 40 hours on a regular basis

    The vacuum sealed pack has been opened (even if not used) they must be replaced after 6 months – the carbon will absorb contaminants from the atmosphere

The expiry date on the cartridge is reached.

Particulate filters get clogged and makes it harder to breath. They should be replaced when:

Breathing becomes difficult
The filters become dirty or get physically damaged.

There are different types of filters or cartridges and the main ones are:

N series – non-resistant to oil

R series – resistant to oil

P series – oil-proof

Cartridges can be identified by the color of the container.

TYPE	COLOUR CODE	DESCRIPTION
An	Orange	Organic vapors and gasses
B	Grey	Inorganic vapors and gasses
E	Yellow	Acid gasses
K	Green	Ammonia
Hg	Red	Mercury

Particulate filters can be identified as follows:

TYPE	DESCRIPTION
P1	Particles generated from mechanical processes such as grinding

P2	Particles from mechanical + thermal processes such as welding
P3	Particles including toxic gasses

Recommendation:

I suggest that you use the 3 M half mask respirator with the orange/brown organic gas and vapor series 6000 cartridge (A type). The type P1 particulate filter is used in conjunction with the series 6000 cartridges.

1.1.3.2 Eye protection.

There are many types of safety glasses but the best for spraying is the type that fits over the face to enclose the sides of the eyes so that contaminant cannot reach any part of the eye. If you wear glasses, you could get safety glasses that fit over your prescription glasses or alternatively use a full face mask that will cover your eyes.

1.1.3.3 Protective clothing

Use overalls to cover your total body. Also use head cover such as a cap to cover your head. Suitable boots that you use for painting only is also essential.

1.1.3.4 Ear protection

When you work with a grinder or sander, wear ear muffs to protect your ears.

1.1.4 Ventilation

Spray painting should only be done in a well ventilated space. It is not advisable to spray outdoors because of dust and bug contamination. If you are going to spray at home and utilize your garage, you could construct a simple spray booth consisting of a framework covered with plastic sheeting on three sides. This will control the overspray in a restricted area and prevent contamination. Also make sure that doors and windows are kept open to ensure a good flow of air. You could also use an electric fan to extract fumes from the interior space but be careful when spraying with oil based paints that have a low combustion level.

1.2 Mixing equipment

Spray painting requires that the paint be accurately mixed so that you get the correct consistency – not too thick and not too thin. Most paint manufacturers give an indication of the ratio of solvent to the paint volume required. As a rule of thumb, 10% solvent is usually sufficient. However, some water based paints are non-drip and comes as a thick liquid that will require a bigger ratio – up to 15%.

Mixing cups are available in the paint trade. These are ideal for accurately measuring the paint mix. Different sizes are available but the 1 liter cups are the most practical. A spray painter's ruler is also a handy measurement and mixing tool.

Most paints used for spray painting must be filtered to get rid of small particles. Paint strainers of various grid sizes are available but the medium mesh size is preferable. Clean paint prevents clogging of nozzles and air holes on the paint gun. Paper strainers can be cleaned and used two or three times before discarding. Reusable paint strainers are also available.

1.3 Brushes and rollers

1.3.1 Brushes

Good quality paint brushes of different sizes will be needed for touch up work, cleaning of dust from the wood etc.

There are basically three types of brushes. Natural hair brushes, synthetic brushes and sponge brushes. Pad applicators can also be regarded as brushes.

The difference between natural and synthetic brushes is like the difference between hair and plastic. Hair becomes uncontrollable when it gets wet but plastic remains workable. It is for this reason that *Natural hair bristle* brushes are preferred for oil based paint and varnishes. *Foam and sponge brushes* are popular because they do not leave brush marks. However, to get a really smooth finish they must be used carefully but with some practice they will give a good result. *Synthetic brushes* are the most versatile of the lot and provided that you get a high quality brush, they can be used to get a good finish.

For small touch ups different type artist brushes do come in handy.

1.3.2 Rollers

Sponge rollers are becoming increasingly popular because they do not leave marks and will give a smooth finish. They are used on flat surfaces but are not effective on round surfaces and edges. To get a smooth finish the roller must be used in one direction only. Do not roll back and forth on the same stroke – rather pick up the roller and start the second stroke from the beginning and roll in one direction.

1.4 Sanding and stripping equipment

Stripping tools are essential for the preparation of the wood surface. It is rare not to strip or sand the old finish before painting.

The following types of sanders are available:

Belt sanders remove a lot of material and must be used with caution. It will leave heavy sanding marks and will need further sanding with an orbital sander and finer sand paper.

Orbital sanders are not as aggressive but also do not remove a lot of material. It still leaves orbital scratches and must be smoothed down with finer grit sand paper. It is only effective when the old finish has started flaking and has dried out completely.

Random orbital sanders have a revolving as well as an orbital movement. They are more effective than orbital sanders and much more effective in removing old finish. This is the best option for most sanding operations.

Other tools to remove old finish include the following:

Heat gun

Two types are available - flame and heat blower. Care must be taken when using a heat gun because it can easily burn the wood and leave burn marks. It is also a messy process and will not entirely remove old finish.

Sand paper

Sandpaper comes in different grades. The grade is based on the number of abrasive particles per square inch that make up the sandpaper. The lower the number, the coarser the grit. It is important to choose the right grit because using a coarse grit can damage the wood or finish.

Coarse – 40 to 60 grit	Medium – 80 to 120 grit
Fine – 150 to 180 grit	Very fine – 220 to 240 grit
Extra fine – 280 to 320 grit	Super fine – 360 and above

Garnet paper is usually a brownish-red or yellow color, which is commonly used in woodworking. It will not sand wood as quickly as other sandpapers, but leaves a better finish. Garnet is an excellent choice for finish sanding.

Aluminum Oxide is another common type of sandpaper for woodworking projects. It is the type of paper most often used in power sanders. Aluminum Oxide is more durable than Garnet paper but doesn't leave such a nice finish on wood surfaces.

Silicon Carbide paper is typically a dark gray or even black. This type of paper is used primarily for finishing metals or for "wet-sanding", using water as a lubricant. While some advanced finishes use Silicon Carbide paper, it is not typically used in woodworking.

When sanding flat surfaces it is much easier to use a sanding block to get an even finish. The final finish should always be with a fine grit to get a smooth finish before painting. Remember, only a smooth surface will ensure a smooth final layer of paint.

Paint scrapers Paint scrapers of different sizes are used fill cracks and holes with wood filler and also to remove old paint or paint stripper to remove paint. Paint scrapers for curved surfaces are also available.

Ordinary pot scrubbers are handy paint stripper tools. They come in various materials such as galvanized wire, copper wire, stainless steel and are available in mesh or spiral form.

A good quality wire brush will remove old paint and paint stripper but should be used with care not to damage the wood.

Tip:

To remove paint stripper first use a paint scraper to remove the bulk and then use a pot scrubber to remove the final remaining bits of stripper, especially in crevices and rounded surfaces. Remember to wipe the wood clean with a wet cloth to neutralize any remaining stripper.

1.5 Maintenance of spray painting equipment

A regular maintenance routine for spray painting tools is vital to ensure that they perform optimally.

1.5.1 Compressor

Try to protect the compressor from excessive paint over spray and dust but make sure that adequate ventilation is available. Follow a regular maintenance program such as the following:

PROCEDURE	FREQUENCY
Check for oil leaks	Daily
Check for vibrations tighten screws	Daily
Check for air leaks	Daily
Check oil level	Weekly
Check filters and clean	Weekly
Check air release valve	Monthly

Drain air tank   Monthly

1.5.2 Spray guns

Spray guns need to be cleaned to prevent nozzles and holes getting clogged up. After each spray session the following must be done:

PROCEDURE	FREQUENCY
Wash paint cup with solvent or water	After spraying
Spray with solvent to clean material passage	After spraying
Wipe cup and lid and open vent hole on lid	After spraying
Remove needle and nozzle and wash	After spraying
Wash gun body with solvent or water	After spraying
Lightly oil springs and needle	Weekly
Lightly oil threads and hinges	Monthly

Tip:

Blow with compressed air to clean and dry body parts. Do not leave paint in the spray gun for more than half an hour. If you are going to spray again within one hour, just empty the paint cup and spray solvent or water for a few seconds to clean material passage ways. There is no need to disassemble the gun.

1.5.3 Good housekeeping

Dust is the number one enemy of spray painting because it settles on the wet paint and leaves a rough surface that can only be fixed by sanding and re-spraying. The spray area should be cleaned every day before spraying. It helps to lightly dampen the floor to keep dust in check. Air extraction and /or good ventilation are essential. For the beginner this can be a costly item but with a bit of ingenuity the problem can be solved. Open doors and windows and use a fan to blow air away from the working area. Do not spray outside.

2. TYPES OF PAINTS, PRIMERS AND SEALERS

Choosing the right kind of paint for furniture is important but this can be difficult because there are so many different types of paint on the market. There is also the choice between water based and oil based paints. Water based paint is also known as Latex or Acrylic paint. Oil based paint is also known as Alkyd paint.

2.1 Oil- and water based paint

Which is the best paint to use for painting furniture? I have painted with both water and oil based paints and although oil based paints gives a nice smooth finish, it has some serious **disadvantages.**

Disadvantages of oil based paint:

White oil paint will tend to turn yellow over time

It does not resist mildew that may form in high humidity areas

It has high VOC (Volatile Organic Compound) and is increasingly being replaced by water based paints

Strong odor that lasts for a long time

It does not "breath" like water based paint and as a result tends to crack, form bubbles or peal.

It has a very long drying time (up to 16 – 24 hours)

Some advantages of oil based or Alkyd paint are the following:

Alkyd goes on smoother than water based paint but takes much longer to dry.

It gives a hard, durable finish that resist scratches and abrasions

Alkyd enamels are easy to wash because the surface is hard and smooth

Alkyd paints are more chemically resistant to stand up to washing detergents than Latex.

Water based paints or Latex (Acrylic) has the following disadvantages:

On new wood, a primer must first be used before painting

It sometimes raises the grain of the wood. This can be overcome by first applying a suitable wood sealer

It does not adhere to chalky surfaces

It cannot readily be painted over surfaces previously painted with oil-based paints. This can be overcome by sealing the old finish first or using a universal undercoat.

Advantages of water based paints are:

Quick drying resulting in better productivity

Virtually no odor and low VOC (volatile organic compound) with less harm to the environment and your health

Paint is flexible and expands with temperature. Will not crack or flake

Equipment can be cleaned with water

Modern water based enamel paint will provide the same smooth, hard finish that could in the past only be achieved by oil paint.

Modern water based paints have been developed to withstand harsh treatment and specialized paints for bathroom furniture, kitchen cabinets, laminates etc. are available. These are up to 10 times more water and scratch resistant than normal Latex paint. I only use water based paint, paint stripper, paint sealer, glaze and wood stain and have never found any defects or problems. Water based paint comes in gloss, semi-gloss and matt finishes. Water based Acrylic enamel paints are widely available and give a tough sheen finish and do not need to be sealed since most have a Polyurethane base for extra durability.

Tip:

For hard working surfaces such as table tops use Acrylic enamel based paints with Polyurethane. Stick to water based paint, sealer, stain etc. Use specialized paint for bathroom furniture, laminates and kitchen cabinets. On previously painted surfaces always apply a universal undercoat first.

2.2 Chalk paint

Chalk paint was made popular by Annie Sloan. It is a paint developed for the DIY market and claims to be very easy to apply and does not need any wood preparation such as sanding or priming. I have been working with chalk paint on a wide variety of wooden surfaces and I have found that you cannot get a good result without properly preparing the wood – especially on old painted wood or where the wood has been damaged. So that to me is not an advantage because there are also other conventional domestic paints that do not need priming before painting, such as the Dulux Made by Me range. It acts as a primer and paint and was specially designed for painting furniture.

Some **disadvantages** of chalk paint are:

Very expensive especially for bigger projects

It must be prepared in the same way as any other paint

It is not that easy to work with because of fast drying property

It must be sealed and this changes the character of the paint – it loses its chalky look.

It is not very suitable for painting hard working surfaces such as tables

Some **advantages** of chalk paint:

Eco-friendly and water based for easy cleaning of tools.

Wonderful range of colors

It can be sprayed with success to get a smooth finish

Ideal for smaller DIY projects

In addition to Annie Sloan wax, a lacquer spray is also available that sprays well and dries to a smooth surface.

Tip:

Make your own chalk paint.

Here is what you will need:

Ultra matt Acrylic paint (paint used for walls and ceilings)

Interior crack filler

Water

Mix the ingredients in a suitable container as follows:

Step 1 – Pour 1 cup of clean water into the container

Step 2 – Slowly add 1 cup of Crack Filler into the water and stir until smooth

Step 3 – Now add 2 cups of paint to the mixture. Add slowly and stir constantly to get a lump free mixture. Add more water if the paint is too thick.

When spraying or brushing chalk paint on old furniture (painted or varnished), I use the following procedure:

Clean the wood with sugar soap to remove dirt

Sand to get a smooth finish (no need to take off all the old paint)

> Seal the wood with a clear water-based sealer.
> Apply top coats (at least 2)

When applying a sealer there is no need for applying a base coat or universal under coat. If yellow spots still show through, apply another coat of sealer and re-paint.

When the final coat is dry, seal with a matt sealer.

To get a smooth finish, sand between coats with 220 grit sand paper.

Because of the nature of chalk paint, it takes some time to get use to working with it.

2.3 Milk paint

Milk paint has been around for a very long time and is extremely durable when cured. Like chalk paint it has become a popular modern trend. It is also an expensive paint and to my mind not suitable for big furniture projects.

Some **disadvantages** of milk paint are the following:

> It comes in a powder form and must be mixed before application
> Once mixed the paint must be used and cannot be stored
> It is expensive when compared with conventional paints
> It cannot be sprayed.

Some **advantages** of milk paint are:

> It is made of natural ingredients and is non-toxic and very safe once applied.
>
> It is ideal for antiquing furniture. Because milk paint does not flow out like conventional paint, it leaves brush marks giving a textured finish to give a genuine antique look.

How to use Milk Paint

Depending on whether it is new wood or previously finished wood, preparation will be needed on old paint and varnished surfaces. A bonding agent must be applied to the first coat to ensure proper adhesion.

The second step is to apply a stain to new wood. The reason is that when you distress by sanding, the stained surface will be exposed giving you the desired aged look.

The mixture for stain is made by mixing three parts of water to one part of Milk Paint powder (any color powder can be used). Stir the mixture well. A thin watery mixture is required and it is applied in even strokes in the direction of the grain. It dries quickly and the next coat can then be applied. The surface can now be painted with the desired top coat.

Milk Paint is mixed as follows:

One part Milk Paint is added to one part water. Add more water if the paint is too thick or more powder if too thin. Stir thoroughly until all the powder is dissolved. Apply the paint evenly and allow 20 to 30 minutes between coats for the paint to dry. At least three coats are required.

When you are satisfied with the coverage, it can be finished by sanding with a fine grit sandpaper. Now apply antique wax or a matt liquid sealer to seal the paint.

Tip:

Make your own Milk Paint.

Here is what you will need.

> ½ Cup of lemon juice or 1 oz of hydrated lime (get from hardware stores)
>
> 1 quart skimmed milk
>
> Sieve
>
> Dry color pigment or matt acrylic paint of the desired color

To prepare the paint the following steps should be followed:

> Mix the lemon juice with the skimmed milk and leave overnight at

room temperature to induce curdling

Pour it through a sieve to separate the liquid from the solids
Add 4 tablespoons of dry color pigment or 4 tablespoons of acrylic paint very slowly to the curd. Stir until the pigment has dispersed throughout the mixture and the desired color is obtained.

Milk paint must be used immediately and just enough must be mixed for use over a short period. When more paint is needed, mix again.

Tip:

Use chalk paint and milk paint for distressing on smaller projects but avoid on bigger projects and hard working surfaces. Do not skip wood preparation on previously finished surfaces. Where sanding does not seem to be required, sand only lightly and seal with a water based sealer before painting.

As an alternative, use ordinary ultra matt acrylic paint (the type used for Painting ceilings) to get the same matt finish. It must be sealed.

2.4 Primers, sealers and undercoats

2.4.1 What is a primer?

Primer is a type of paint that has been developed specifically as a first coat to be applied to a bare substrate. Primer is probably the most important coat of paint on any bare surface. The final paint cover depends on the primed surface to do its job properly.

Before applying a primer the surface must be smooth and clean. All dust particles must be removed and the wood must be dry.

The main functions of primers are the following:

To provide adhesion to the substrate so that the top coat sticks properly

To provide a protective coating to the wood surface until it can be painted with a top coat. Some primers also provide a UV block to protect wood from the sun

To restrict any moisture from reaching the wood surface and the growth of mould.

Some primers have distinct colors to distinguish it from other paint.

2.4.2 What is a sealer?

The functions of sealers and primers can overlap and in some cases it is better to use a sealer instead of a primer. A sealer can be used prior or in place of a primer. In a sense one can say that sealers are special types of primers. Some of the functions of sealers are the following:

It helps to provide a good adhesive surface for the top coat

It seals off surface porosity to prevent paint from sinking in causing uneven coverage

It blocks stains and seepage of oils and resin from the wood.

Sanding sealer has a particular function on new sanded surfaces. It seals exposed wood grain and provides a smooth surface for painting. A sealer can be used instead of a primer.

2.4.3 What is an undercoat?

Undercoats are used to paint over the primer or sealer and their functions are:

To provide adhesion to the primed surface

To provide a base for the top coat to stick to

In some cases the undercoat will do the same job as a primer

To fill imperfections in the surface thus providing a smooth surface to paint on.

Tip:

When painting new wood a good universal undercoat will perform the function of a primer. On previously painted surfaces first apply an

undercoat and if seepage occurs, seal the wood with a clear sealer before applying the top coat.
Tip:

Before painting a previously painted piece of furniture, first determine what type of paint was used. **The reason is that you can paint oil based paint over water based but never the other way around.** Brown spots will show and the Latex will not adhere properly.

To test the paint take a piece of cotton wool and place some rubbing alcohol (or nail polish remover)on it and rub the surface. If some paint rubs off you know that it is water based paint.

3. HOW TO PREPARE WOOD FOR PAINTING

Before painting any wood surface (whether new or old painted or varnished wood), it must be properly prepared. The first step is to clean the wood and then to do repairs and filling cracks, scratches etc. with wood filler.

3.1 Repairs

More often than not, old pieces of furniture need at least minor repairs. In some cases parts are broken so badly that it must be replaced. Making new parts cannot be considered part of the refinishing process. This should be left to furniture makers.

Before any repairs can be done all hardware should be removed – locks, handles, hinges and metal beadings. Next the item should be properly cleaned. If necessary, a solution of warm water and sugar soap should be used to wash the wood. Use a firm brush to remove grease and dirt. Rinse with clean water and let the wood dry out completely before working on it. Next repairs can be done.

3.1.1 Fixing cracks and holes

Sometimes cracks may occur and depending on the extent it affects the construction of the piece, can be repaired with wood glue and clamping it for a few hours. If the crack is small, it can be fixed with wood filler. Fill up higher than the surrounding surface and sand down when dry. When the item must be varnished rather than painted, wood filler can be problematic because the color seldom matches the original finish. Try to get some wood shavings that match the original finish and mix with wood glue. Insert it into the crack and when it is dry, sand to a smooth finish.

Where bigger cracks or chips in the wood must be filled, it is best to use a wood epoxy such as Quick Wood. It can also be sanded to a fine finish and will not chip or wear off.

3.1.2 Repairing drawers

In many old cabinets the drawers do not work properly and this can in most cases be fixed without major effort. The mechanism for opening a drawer can include rollers (mostly in kitchen cabinets), runners at the bottom of the drawer and a groove on the sides of the drawer that accommodates a wooden guide that runs in the opening.

Most common problems found in drawers are the following:

>Drawer keeps sliding out

>It won't close properly

>Drawer bottom is sagging or broken

>Drawer frame joints loose

>Drawer won't slide

When a drawer keeps falling out it usually do not have a stop at the back of the drawer. To fix the problem, cut a piece of hardwood and fasten it to the back of the drawer. Swing it away to insert the drawer and then fix the stop block with a second nail or screw.

Drawers that do not want to close or get stuck can have several problems such as:

Loose joints

Drawers are put together by using dovetail joints or butt joints. Dovetail joints seldom separate. If they do become loose, force some wood glue into the joint and clamp firmly together. Butt joints usually need more attention. Try and take the joint apart and after cleaning it properly, glue and clamp. If possible you can nail the joint to give extra strength.

Sticky drawers

This can be caused by the runners that may need lubricating with stick lubricant, candle wax or silicone sprays. Do not use ordinary oil since it collects dust and worsens the problem. If lubrication does not help, sand down the binding points. Seal the raw wood with shellac to prevent future swelling.

Worn guides and runners

Wood or metal runners are used to guide drawers to move in and out. When they are worn or splintering they must be smoothed out with sandpaper or they must be replaced. Metal guides that can be bought at any hardware store can be installed. You could also replace the runners with new wooden runners. Use hardwood to make the runner. Secure it with glue and nails. Countersink the nails so they won't interfere with the drawer's movement.

Worn drawer bottoms

Drawer bottoms are usually fixed to the frame by slots in the sides of the drawer into which the bottom slides in loosely. To replace a drawer bottom, remove one end of the drawer and slide out the bottom panel. Replace it with new hardboard or hardwood panel cut to size.

Some drawer bottoms are secured with moldings or corner blocks at the inside edges of the sides and back of the drawer. Remove these before taking out the bottom.

3.1.3 Fixing legs on chairs and tables

When a leg is broken, it is difficult to repair and most of the time should be replaced with a new leg. However, when the leg joint is loose, it can be repaired by taking the joints apart and then re-gluing the joints. Alternatively, a dowel can be inserted to connect the leg with the adjoining part of the table. Corner blocks can also be fastened in the corners under the table top to strengthen the joint of the leg to the table frame.

3.2 Preparing different wood surfaces

There are some differences in preparing new wooden surfaces and previously panted or stained wood surfaces.

3.2.1 New wood surfaces

New wood obviously does not need as much attention as previously finished wood but there are still some steps to be taken before painting can start. There are also different steps for hard wood, manufactured wood such as MDF, chip board and veneered wood.

3.2.2 Hard wood surfaces

The main point with hard wood is that natural wood oils and resin must be prevented from seeping through to the painted surface. It is also important to seal knots and to prevent moisture from penetrating the wood surface. In general the following steps should be taken:

Make sure that the wood is clean and dry and that there are no stains or oily patches on the wood surface.

Fill any damaged areas with wood filler.

Seal knots with knot sealer.

Sand the wood to a smooth finish. Start off with a 220 grit and finish with a 350 grit or higher. Clean with a damp cloth to remove wood dust.

If the wood feels slightly rough under touch apply a sanding sealer. When dry sand with a 220 grit sand paper.

The surface is now ready for applying the wood primer and undercoat. Sand between coats with 220 grit sandpaper.

Before applying top coats the primed surface must be given ample time (12 to 16 hours) to dry completely. Sand with 220 grit sandpaper before applying top coats.

3.2.3 Engineered wood surfaces

Medium density fiber board (MDF) is an engineered wood product. Wood fibers are combined with resin binder and compressed into boards under high pressure and temperature. These boards are used in furniture and cabinet manufacture because it has a very smooth surface free from knots and other imperfections. Because of its smoothness it is ideal for spray painting. Before spraying it must be sanded with a fine sandpaper to get a clean surface. The exposed sides of the board are very porous and must first be sealed with a sealer to prevent the paint from sinking into the wood.

Tip:

Add a small amount of water to wood filler and mix to a thick liquid form (about as thick as a thick cream) and apply with a paint brush to cover all the edges of the wood. When dry, sand lightly to a smooth surface. An undercoat or primer can now be applied before painting top coats.

Plywood is made up of a number of thin wood layers bonded together by a special adhesive. It is used more generally in the building industry but can also be veneered to give a more durable and attractive wooden board. Before painting sand to a smooth finish. Apply one coat of wood primer and then apply an undercoat before applying the top coats.

Veneer is usually made of a very thin layer of hardwood. This layer is then bonded to a cheaper particle board and can be finished showing the wood grain or it can be painted. It can be sanded and refinished but because it is such a thin layer of hardwood, care must be taken not to sand through to the particle board. First fill scratches etc with wood filler before sanding lightly to a smooth finish. Apply a universal undercoat.

Laminate is made up of synthetic materials or thin slices of wood. It has a shiny finish resembling a plastic surface. It is cheap to produce and is used for the manufacture of low-end furniture. It can be painted, but a special primer must be used to ensure the paint sticks to the surface. The glossy finish must first be sanded to remove the shine before applying the primer.

3.3 Previously painted surfaces

Although there are some instances where very little preparation is needed, it is critical to properly prepare the wood to get a smooth, professional finish. Remember that no matter how well you apply the paint it will not conceal the imperfections in the wood surface and about 80 % of the time should be spent on preparation and only about 20% on the actual painting.

The following procedure should be followed when preparing previously painted or varnished surfaces. The preparation will largely depend on two factors. Firstly, whether the old finish was oil- or water based and whether the new paint will be oil- or water based. Secondly, the condition of the existing finishes and in this case the older the item the more likely it is that the old finish will have to be removed all together.

3.3.1 Oil based finishes

When the existing finish is oil based, and you are going to use an oil based paint to refinish the item, all that you really need to do is to clean it properly and to sand the wood to a smooth finish and then to apply the top coat.

However, when you are going to use water based paint such as Acrylic/Latex or chalk paint then more care should be taken to prevent oils from seeping through the top coat to form yellow/brown spots. The following steps can be taken:

> Start by washing the object with a solution of sugar soap and water. Brush it on and give it some time to soften the dirt and grime. Then take a clean cloth and wipe down the surface.
>
> Sand down with a 220 grit sandpaper to remove the shiny appearance and then apply a universal under coat (at least 2 coats).
>
> Now apply the first top coat. When there is no seepage the second coat can be applied. When seepage occurs, apply a clear water based sealer and then apply the top coat. This should stop seepage.

3.3.2 Water based finishes

When the old finish is water based then all that is necessary is to clean it with sugar soap and then to apply the top coat. Where the old finish is in poor condition, it should be sanded to a smooth surface before painting.

3.4 Stripping old finishes

There are a number of ways to strip the old paint or varnish finish from wood.

> Strip by sanding by hand or a sander

Strip with chemical stripper

Strip with heat.

3.4.1 Sanding

Sanding to remove old finish or to prepare the wood for painting is an important step in the refinishing process. It is important to use the correct sand paper. A wrong choice can damage the wood surface and make it difficult to repair.

The general approach to sanding is to start with a coarser grit and then move to a finer grit to remove grit marks left by the coarser sandpaper.

Sanding can be done mechanically or by hand. Mechanical sanding is sometimes unavoidable. Small area such as arm rests, table legs and edges must be sanded by hand.

When sanding flat areas by hand it is always better to use a sanding block - always sand in the direction of the wood grain. Once the old finish has been removed, the wood must be smoothed with finer sand paper. I like to start sanding with a 150 grit, then move to 220 grit to smooth the wood grain.

When buying sand paper, be aware that you can get dry and wet paper. For paint removal the dry paper seems to be more effective. The cabinet paper in orange is mostly used on wood.

3.4.2 Chemical stripper

This is the most efficient way of stripping old paint or varnishes. There are two types available – solvent based and water based. The water based stripper has many advantages over the oil based strippers. Some of these are:

It does not severely irritate the skin or eyes

Equipment can be cleaned with water

I prefer to use a water based stripper. It is effective and has virtually no odor. It can easily be washed off with water. It has the following features:

> A thick gel formulation that clings to vertical surfaces.
> Bio degradable.
> Water based.
> Non flammable.
> Contains no ethylene chloride.
> Safe, effective, and easy to use.

The stripper is liberally applied with a brush to cover a manageable area. After about 15 minutes, stripping can start and the most effective way is to first use a paint scraper to remove the bulk of the stripper. Follow up by removing the remaining stripper with a pot scrubber and water.

You might have to repeat the process a few times by brushing the liquid on and after 10 – 20 minutes scraping it off. When the process is finished, the stripper must be neutralized by rinsing it down with clean water. When the wood is completely dry you can start with the sanding process. You might find that the wood grain has been raised and to rectify this, the wood must first be treated with a sanding sealer and then sanded down to a smooth finish.

Remember that all chemical strippers can be harmful to your health. So it's best to use gloves, eye protection and a suitable mask.

Stripping of old finish is a most important step in the process of refinishing. If you do not do this properly, the end result will be bad and in most cases this means that you have to start the process all over again. Once the old paint or varnish is removed the next step is to sands it to a smooth finish – as smooth as possible. Therefore, start with 220 grit sanding paper and finish off with 880 or even 1000 grit. Wipe dust completely and inspect for sanding marks or other blemishes that may remain.

There is another option which does not involve stripping the old finish before you start painting. Provided that the existing finish is still in good shape and does not crack, peel or make bubbles. Take the following steps:

> Clean the wood by washing with sugar soap to remove dirt and

grease. Wash down with clean water and let it dry.
Sand lightly with 220 grit sandpaper

Seal the wood with a clear water based sealer

When dry, paint with a water based paint.

This process is especially successful where the old finish is oil based paint or any lacquer or varnish finish. When you do not seal it first, the water based paint over the oil based paint will result in yellow stains that may appear. To resolve this problem, you can seal the paint and then repaint in the surface again. This should remove the stains.

3.4.3 Using Heat Guns

Basically there are two tools available for stripping paint with heat – heat gun and blow torch. The main difference is that the blow torch has an open flame whereas the heat gun heats air that is blown over the wood.

Blow torches are much more aggressive and must be used with care to avoid scourging or burning the wood.

When using either tool ensure that it is held a constant distance from the surface, roughly 6 to 8 inches from the surface. Move the gun backwards and forwards in a sweeping motion. Do not keep the gun stationery on one spot to avoid overheating and scourging the wood. When the paint starts to wrinkle and lift from the surface, it must be removed with a paint scraper. Keep an old container such as an empty tin handy to discard the melted paint.

Repeat the process until all the paint is removed. Use a 220 grit sand paper to remove remaining paint residue and make sure that the surface is clean and smooth before painting.

Remember that the heat can be dangerous when it comes in contact with flammable substances such as thinners. Oil based paints may also give off harmful gases and it is preferable to use a mask, gloves and eye protection.

Advantages:

It can remove paint very quickly

It works on multiple layers

It is relatively cheap

Disadvantages:

It can be very dangerous

It can damage the surface or item you are trying to strip especially wood surfaces

It may need several different tools to complete the job.

Use heat stripping with care and unless manual sanding or electric sanders are unsuccessful, try and avoid heat gins.

4. SPRAY PAINTING BASICS

Applying paint or other finish such as varnish, takes some practice to achieve a professional result. The best method of applying paint is the use of a spray gun. The spray technique can easily be mastered, provided that the right procedures are followed.

4.1 How to spray paint.

Proper spraying techniques are very logical. Some of the basic principles for quality spraying are the following:

> Plan a systematic spraying routine that will reduce waste and overspray. I start on the underside of a piece of furniture. On a chair for instance, tip it over and start with the legs and the bottom. Then turn it over and start from the top by spraying the back, armrests etc. Lastly spray the seat. Always work from top to bottom and the inside to the outside. Work from the less visible to the more visible areas.

> Make sure that you have adequate light. Keep the spray gun pointed perpendicular to the surface of the wood. Avoid movements of the wrist. Move the whole arm from left to right.

> Set your gun to a fan pattern that covers the surface with the fewest passes and the least overspray. Use a small fan pattern on edges, rails, turnings, and other narrow surfaces. Use a wide fan pattern on large, wide surfaces.

> Start spraying about 4-6 inches from the side of the wood, and move the spray onto the wood. Keep moving at a uniform speed.

Keep the gun a uniform distance from the surface of the wood between 6 and 10 inches. If you move it too close, you will make runs; move it too far away, and you will have dry spray. You usually have to hold an HVLP gun several inches closer to the wood than you do a conventional gun.

Finish your stroke several inches past the edge of the wood. Make it a habit to release the trigger of the gun at the end of each stroke.

Make sure that the strokes overlap to ensure even thickness. Also spray each stroke at least two times - one stroke to the edge and back on the same stroke. Overlap each previous stroke by half. This will give an even thickness overall.

Avoid spraying to much the first time around. Running of the paint may occur and then you will have to redo the whole process. Rather spray several coats to make sure you have adequate coverage.

Remember, practice makes perfect. Don't expect to be an expert spray painter after the first couple of efforts.

First spray a test stroke on a piece of scrap to make sure the spray pattern is correct and the volume of air and material is adequate. After spraying a few strokes, stop spraying and stand away and have a look against the light to see if the painted surface is shiny and that it does not appear like a matt finish. If the latter is the case, not enough paint is deposited and it must be corrected by doing one of the following:

> Make sure the paint is not too thick and the volume of air and paint release is sufficient.

> Make sure the paint nozzle on the gun is open and not blocked by impurities.

> Close the paint volume knob and spray to remove impurities. If this does not help, the cup must be emptied and the gun taken apart and cleaned.

4.2 How to mix the paint

Another important skill that is required for proper spraying is the ability to properly mix the paint. In most cases the commercial paints are thick (especially water based paint) and need to be thinned to achieve a good flow of paint through the gun. Mixing takes a bit of practice. Water based paint can be thinned up to 10% or even more. A paint measuring cup clearly indicates the 10% scale and should preferably be used. A spray painter's ruler can also be used. Always spray a test stroke to make sure that the right amount of paint is deposited.

Most Acrylic paints must be thinned down to get the right consistency (thickness). Depending on the brand of paint you might have to do some experimenting to achieve the right consistency.

After thinning, the paint must be filtered through a paint strainer to remove impurities. There are different types of strainers but the most popular are nylon mesh or paper funnel strainers.

Tip:

You can make your own reusable paint strainer from the same strainer material that can be bought from a paint dealer. The 20 liter strainer can be cut up into smaller pieces to fit around the opening of a mixing cup. Use a piece of elastic to secure the mesh over the cup. Pour the paint and then detach and wash the mesh for future use.

4.3 Setting up spray painting equipment

4.3 1 Spray gun settings

Always make sure that you have the correct setting on your gun for the amount of air that goes through the nozzle. The combination of air and paint is called atomization. The gun shoots a stream of paint that is broken up in a mist of tiny droplets that is deposited on the wood. If you have too little air, the atomization won't be great enough, and the finish won't flow together. It will cure looking like the surface of an orange; the effect is called orange peel. If you have too much air, the finish will dry before it hits the wood, producing a dusty matt look. This is called dry spray.

The two air jets that direct the atomizing air have an additional function. They determine the width of the paint fan by forcing the air on the stream of paint. By increasing the air flow through these jets, you widen the fan, so you can coat a wider area with each pass. By decreasing the airflow, you shrink the fan to a very small circular pattern, which you can use to fill in small defects. By rotating the air nozzle, you can change the angle of the fan (vertical or horizontal) relative to the gun.

Before setting the spray gun, read the manufacturer's instructions and make sure that the correct settings are used. There are three settings that should be set before spraying.

Firstly, the air supply knob is usually located at the bottom of the handle and controls the amount of air passing through to the nozzle. Close the knob and open it with one turn of the knob. This will provide a normal volume of air but test it by spraying on a piece of wood to see if the paint sprays evenly and enough paint is deposited on the wood to give a shiny surface. Some spray guns have a pressure gauge and the air pressure can be set to the required level.

Secondly, the paint regulating knob regulates the amount of paint that passes through the gun. Too much pant will make the paint to run and too little paint will result in a dry spray. Do a test run and start by closing the paint regulating knob. Now open with one turn and spray to check the amount of paint deposited. Adjust further if necessary.

Thirdly, there is a knob to adjust the paint fan that leaves the nozzle. Test to set the fan to a length of about 5 inches or 80 cm. This is the width that is used when spraying a flat surface. The fan is reduced when edges or corners are sprayed.

The correct setting of the spray gun involves the correct volume of paint being passed through the nozzle by the correct volume of air. Together with the width of the fan it should leave enough paint on the surface to provide a shiny layer of paint. Remember that at least two coats of paint will be required so do not try and get a 100% coverage the first time around.

4.3.2 How to set the air compressor

Most small compressors have two gauges. The first measures the air pressure in the tank and the second the air pressure released at the air outlet. There is also an air regulating knob to regulate the air flow. It is important to set the air at the correct settings for the spray gun to function optimally. If your HVLP gun requires 12 cfm air delivery at 45 psi the compressor must be able to produce that amount of pressurized air.

If your gun is specified to operate at 3 bar, start by setting the regulating gauge to 4 bar. Now connect the gun and while spraying (without paint) note the drop in pressure on the pressure gauge. If it drops below 3 bar turn the regulating knob to increase the pressure to 5 bar. Repeat the test with the gun and when it is stable on 3 bar, tighten the regulating knob.

The air pressure should be checked periodically to ensure a stable air supply.

4.4 Where to Spray

You can spray in a garage with the doors open. The best setup for indoors is a spray booth, which exhausts the air through a filter that catches all the solid finish particles. It is preferable not to use an electric fan when working with oil based paints, lacquer or varnishes. The sparks from the motor might ignite lacquer and varnish fumes; also, the solid particles from your overspray will build up on the fan's electrical components, increasing the fire hazard.

I started off in my garage and within a year I had to get a bigger work place. I approached a local cabinet maker and suggested that I set up a facility at the back of his shop and that I would do spray painting for him. This was agreed and I then bought a second hand ship container and converted it into a spray booth. Although the space is small, it is sufficient for spraying. Other activities such as sanding and washing can be done outside.

4.5 Organizing the work

Before you start spraying decide how to approach the spray sequence. As said earlier, start from the inside out and do the inaccessible areas first. Make sure that you can reach all the areas on the work piece without the risk of damaging already painted areas.

Try and handle the work piece as little as possible. Use a work horse and scaffold planks as a bench to place the item at a convenient height to reach all the difficult places. Let the work piece become touch-dry before you handle it. It is also important to make sure that no dust or insects come into contact with the work piece before the paint is touch-dry.

Tip:

On flat surfaces that have to be painted on both sides (like cabinet doors), you have three options;

1. Place on a flat work surface and spray one side and wait until the paint has dried and then spray the other side. This is a lengthy process and the next two options will reduce work time dramatically.

2. Use paint pyramids (obtainable from hardware stores and paint dealers) to suspend the work piece. Spray one side and wait a few minutes for the paint to settle and then turn it around to do the other side. Be careful to touch the edges only.

3. On flat items use small nails and drive them halfway into the edges of two opposite sides of the work piece. Use two nails for each side. Place the work piece with the nailed edges on two blocks the same width as the work piece to suspend it from the work surface. The nailed edges keep the work piece suspended and the one side can be painted. Wait a minute or two for the paint to settle and turn it around by using the nails as handles. Take care not to touch the painted surface.

4.6 Maintenance and cleaning of equipment

One of the most important aspects in being a good spray painter is to get in the routine of good housekeeping. Always keep the area free of dust. You could even spray water on the floor surface to settle dust. Make sure that the piece is clean and free from dust particles. Run the palm of your hand over the surface. You will immediately feel dust and rough patches. Get into the habit of wiping the surface with a clean cloth before spraying or even better, use your compressor to blow away dust.

Cleaning paint equipment such as the spray gun is critically important. After each spray session, disassemble the gun totally and clean out with the substance recommended by the paint manufacturer (water, thinners or mineral turpentine). It is especially important with water based paint. Once this paint is cured water will not clean it and thinners will have to be used. If you have a gravity fed gun make sure that you also clean the breathing hole in the lid of the cup.

4.7 How to use a spray can

When using a spray can the same basic principles apply to using an air gun. It is very straight forward provided you do the following:

Shake the can well before starting

Use the same smooth motions from left to right

Keep the can about 6 inches away from the object

Do not over spray. Spray three thin coats to get proper coverage

Tip:

To clear the nozzle after spraying, turn the can upside down and spray to remove the paint from the nozzle.

Using a paint handle that fits over the can makes control of the spraying much easier.

4.8 How to use brushes and rollers

Different rollers should be used for water and oil based paints. For the best result the synthetic rollers are used for water based paints and natural fibers like wool or mohair for oil based paint. In general, smoother surfaces require a shorter nap (material covering the roller) and rougher surfaces require a longer nap. Sponge rollers are becoming increasingly popular because they do not leave marks and will give a smooth finish. They are used on flat surfaces but are not effective on round surfaces and edges. To get a smooth finish the roller must be used in one direction only. Do not roll back and forth on the same stroke – rather pick up the roller and start the second stroke from the beginning and roll in one direction. Good quality paint brushes of different sizes are used for touch up work, cleaning of dust from the wood etc.

There are basically three types of brushes. Natural hair brushes, synthetic brushes and sponge brushes. Pad applicators can also be regarded as brushes. They come in different sizes and are handy when doing paint techniques such as dragging or painting stripes.

The difference between natural and synthetic brushes is like the difference between hair and plastic. Hair becomes uncontrollable when it gets wet but plastic remains workable. It is for this reason *Natural hair bristle* brushes are preferred for oil based paint and varnishes. *Foam and sponge brushes* are popular because they do not leave brush marks. However, to get a really smooth finish they must be used carefully but with some practice they will give a good result. *Synthetic brushes* are the most versatile of lot and provided that you get a high quality brush, they can be used to get a good finish.

5. HOW TO SPRAY PAINT DIFFERENT WOOD SURFACES

The biggest difference in painting different wood surfaces has to do with the preparation of the wood. It depends on whether it is an old piece of furniture or new wood. There is also a difference in preparing engineered wood and laminated surfaces such as kitchen cabinets.

5.1 Painting old furniture

As a general rule the following steps should be followed when painting old furniture:

Step 1 – Clean and sand

Mix sugar soap with warm water and wash down the work piece. When dry start to remove old finish. Test with 150 grit sand paper to see if the finish can be removed easily. If not, you might have to use a chemical paint stripper to do the job. Where the old finish is still in a good condition, it is not necessary to remove all the finish. Just remove the gloss and then use a finer sand paper (such as 220 grit) to smooth down the surface. Wipe the wood with a damp cloth to remove the dust.

Step 2 – Fill cracks and holes

Use wood filler to fill holes and cracks. Bigger holes could be filled with wood epoxy to provide a stronger patch. Sand it to a smooth finish. This step might be repeated when the under coat is applied because small scratches and dents will then be more visible.

Step 3 – Seal and prime

When painting with water based paint, it is important to first seal the wood to avoid yellow stains seeping through when you apply the paint. Use water based clear sealer. When dry, sand with a 220 grit sand paper and then apply a multi-purpose undercoat. The work piece should now be ready to apply the first top coat. Remember to sand the undercoat with 220 grit sand paper.

Step 5– Apply top coats (at least 2)

Water based enamel paint is ideal to use as a furniture paint. Some brands are thicker and are non-drip. Whatever the case, the paint should be thinned with water (10%) to make it easier to apply. Do not try and cover the wood in one thick coat. Rather put on 2 or 3 thinner coats and you will get a much smoother finish. Also remember to sand with 220 grit sand paper between coats.

5.2 Painting new wood surfaces

New wood does not need sealing but must be primed before painting. With Pine furniture, the wood knots must first be sealed with a knot sealer. This prevents wood oil seeping through to the paint.

With new furniture the following general steps should be followed:

Step 1 – Sand and seal where necessary

Do not skip the sanding even if the wood surface seems smooth. Use a finer grit to get it as smooth as possible. Seal pine wood with knot seal. Sanding sealer can be used to seal timber grain. It is also good grain filler and can be used as a base coat before applying the top coats.

Step 2 – Apply primer and/or universal under coat

Wood primer penetrates and seals the wood. It provides a strong bond for subsequent coats. The disadvantage is that it is slow drying and takes 16 hours before it can be over coated. It is also toxic and must handle with care. Eye and hand protection is necessary as well as good ventilation. I find that in most cases a good undercoat to be sufficient and use a primer only where the wood is very porous but sanding sealer can also do the job.

Universal undercoat acts as a sandwich coat between the primer and top coats. It is used on both new wood and previously painted surfaces.

Multi-surface undercoat is water-based and is ideal when used in conjunction with water-based top coats. It is fast drying and contains no lead or harmful chemicals. It can be over coated with Alkyd or water-based paints. It can be used on new and previously painted surfaces. I recommend the use of multi-purpose under coat/primer for furniture and cabinets (including Melamine/laminate surfaces).

Step 3 – Apply top coats

This is the same as for previously painted surfaces. Apply at least two coats and sand lightly with a 220 grit paper between coats. After the final coat the work piece must not be handled or moved before it is touch-dry. Make sure that dust does not come into contact with the wet surface.

5.3 Painting kitchen cabinets

5.3.1 New wood cabinets

New hardwood cabinets are treated in much the same way as any piece of furniture. The same process is followed. The process starts with preparing the wood by smoothing it to a fine finish first. Then a sanding sealer or primer is applied. The next step is a suitable multi-surface undercoat; where after two top coats are applied.

It is important to use the correct type of paint because it requires a hard wearing paint to withstand rough handling as well as moisture, heat and scratches. Some major paint manufacturers have specific brands for kitchens and bathrooms. Water-based enamel paint is recommended for kitchen cabinets. This is a tough enamel paint that contains a polyurethane hybrid that prevents chipping and peeling. It is scratch resistant and completely washable. It is antibacterial and prevents fungus growth.

5.3.2 Previously painted kitchen cabinets

Refinishing old kitchen cabinets can be very rewarding because it is much cheaper than new cabinets and when done properly, looks great.

The process includes the following steps:

Step 1 – Remove doors and drawers and clean

Remember to number the doors before removing them – putting them back will be much easier. Remove handles and hinges and wash them with a mixture of sugar soap and warm water to remove grease and dirt. Rinse with clean water to neutralize the sugar soap.

Step 2 – Sand old finish

Where the old finish is still in a good condition, it is not necessary to remove it all together but it is necessary to sand it down to a smooth finish and to break the shiny gloss to a matt finish. Start by using a 100 grit sand paper and follow it up with a finer 220 grit.

Step 3 – Apply undercoat

Apply a multi-purpose undercoat. Sand down to a fine finish with 220 grit sandpaper.

Step 4 – Apply top coats

Apply two coats of water-based enamel paint.

5.3.3 Laminated cabinets

Laminated (Melamine) cabinets can be painted with great success. The following steps can be followed:

Step 1 – Remove all the doors and drawers and start by removing the hardware and then cleaning it with a strong sugar soap solution. Neutralize the sugar soap by wiping it with a clean cloth soaked in clean water.

Step 2 – Lightly sand the doors and drawer fronts with a fine (220 grit) sand paper. Clean it with a damp cloth to remove dust. Remember to sand in the direction of the grain.

Step 3 – Apply a multi-purpose primer. Special primers are available for use on laminate, tiles etc.

Step 4 – When dry, sand down the primer lightly with 220 grit sandpaper. Let it stand overnight to cure properly.

Step 5 – Apply at least two top coats of suitable water-based enamel paint.

Step 6 – Before replacing the doors, first paint the fixed units and make sure that all visible sections are painted. Use a high quality foam roller and follow the same procedure as described above.

When choosing paint for kitchen and bathroom cabinets, choose a specialized paint that can withstand high humidity and steam. Most of these paints also inhibit microbial growth, mould and mildew. It must also be washable and easy to clean.

5.4 How to stain wood

It is sometimes necessary to re-varnish a piece of furniture rather than to paint. This is especially true for antiques and some hardwood pieces such as Stinkwood and Yellow wood. Many people prefer to keep the piece looking the same as the original. When the old finish has deteriorated and faded it is necessary to remove the old finish and start from scratch.

It is important to understand the difference between a stain, varnish and sealer.

A **sealer** penetrates into the wood and allows it to breathe and expand. It is not necessary to remove a sealer before painting the wood.

A **varnish** forms a thin layer on the wood and does not penetrate. Old varnish must be removed totally before applying a new finish. It can be matt or gloss.

A **stain** colors the wood. It does not provide any protection to the wood and must be sealed or painted to provide protection.

There are basically two types of stains – gel and liquid. They can also be water or oil-based   stains. The main reason for staining wood is to change or enhance the color:

> Pine furniture can be turned into rich dark wood colors
> Light woods can become dark woods
> The color of weathered wood can be enhanced.

Gel stains are easy to apply. Use a lint free cloth or sponge to wipe on the wood. Liquid stains can be applied with a cloth or a brush. To get a darker shade, apply more coats. Use a plastic glove to protect your hands. Remember that the stain does not protect the wood. When it is completely dry, finish it off with the application of a Polyurethane water-base sealer.

5.5 How to apply varnish and sealers to wood

Applying varnish and sealers is very straight forward. Just follow the manufacturer's instructions on the container. Always work in the direction of the grain. The surface must be well sanded, clean and free from dirt and grease. The best way to apply a varnish is to spray it. This gives a smooth, professional finish. Most varnishes are quick drying. At least two to three coats are required.

Varnishes come in different colors and are also available as a clear coating. They are also available in water-based or oil-based products.

A wide variety of sealers are available and I would recommend using a clear water-based sealer with a Polyurethane base. They are available in matt, gloss or sheen finish. I prefer the sheen finish for furniture.

6. RESOURCES

Should you require more information on the topics discussed in this book, I have listed a view websites I found useful.

www./spraysafer.qld.gov.au

Although this website is aimed at the Australian spray painting industry, it has useful information on safety issues. There is a specific section dealing with personal protective equipment (PPE) that has good information on personal safety.

www./painters.edu.au

Another Australian website dealing with topics such as using a spray gun, safety considerations and paint decorating tools and equipment.

www./popular mechanics.com

More information on how to spray paint.

www./instructables.com

How to spray with a spray can.

www.gopaintsprayer.com

Comparison of handheld airless spray guns.

www.artofmanliness.com

A useful guide for doing basic furniture repairs.

7. CONCLUSION

Although there will always be a need for paint brushes and rollers for special applications, spray painting makes painting so much faster and the end result so much more professional that serious furniture redecorators should seriously consider it as normal practice. Spray painting can be fun and there are paint sprayers ranging from a simple spray can to the more advanced handheld electric sprayers and compressed air sprayers. By using the correct safety gear, the right spray equipment and eco-friendly water based paints; it is safe and easy to master.

Printed in Great Britain
by Amazon